About the Author

The author has always had a soft spot for nature, and admires views and the beauty of a place. She writes with all that in mind. Susan started writing what she sees or does, whatever comes to mind. Some of her inspirational poems have developed from these trips. The author has always had pleasure from writing these poems. They give her a lot of fulfillment, which gives her the inspiration to carry on. Susan hopes that her poems will give a lot of enjoyment as the things they describe have given her. A lot of effort has been put into making this. Every possible detail has been added to give an insight to the makings of the poems.

Dedication

I dedicate this book to my late husband Ray and late mum Joan.

Sadly missed.

Susan Francis

POEMS TO INSPIRE

AUSTIN MACAULEY PUBLISHERS™
LONDON • CAMBRIDGE • NEW YORK • SHARJAH

A CIP catalogue record for this title is available from the British Library.

ISBN 9781528934893 (Paperback)
ISBN 9781528934909 (Hardback)
ISBN 9781528968065 (ePub e-book)

www.austinmacauley.com

First Published (2021)
Austin Macauley Publishers Ltd
25 Canada Square
Canary Wharf
London
E14 5LQ

Acknowledgements

I would like to thank my daughter Jo, for being there when I needed her the most.

Poems

Love of My Life 13
Faithful Friend 13
Wedding Day 14
Baby Girl 14
Hurry Scurry 15
Rockabye Baby 15
Dear Friend 16
A Special Friendship 16
Runaway Train 17
Mouse on the Go 17
Trusted Friend 18
The King 18
Game's Up 19
Little Baby 19
Having a Tough Day 20
My Prince Charming 20
Achieving Something 21
Worshipping You 21
Little Treasure 21
My Lover 22
Little Star 22
Remembering You 23
A Drama Queen 23
Loving You 24
Beautiful Rose 24
In Our Thoughts 25
Piggy Porker 25
A Tribute 26
Tammy 26
Going a Distance 27
Letting Off Steam 27
Being Happy 28
My Grandson 28
The Terrors 29
Bonfire Night 29
Dear Grandad 30
Up to Tricks 30
Always You 31
Lord 31
Christmas Day 32
Mr. Loveable 32
All United 33
A Sweetheart 33
Night Before Christmas 34
A Day of Fishing 34
The Wonder of the World 35
The Festivities Have Begun 35
A Busy Santa 36
Little Princess 36
A Big Sleep 37
Mouse Hunter 37
Bonfire Frenzy 38
A Day of It 38
Fighting the Enemy 39
Hay-Ho for Santa 39
Little Angel 40
Time to Go 40
A Restless Tot 41
Miss Charming 41
A Believer 42
A Special Day 42

Joy 43
Dreaming of a Peaceful Day 43
June 44
A Happy Day 44
Thinking Back 45
Keeping Together 45
My Girl 46
The Time of Your Life 46
Naughty Puppy 47
A Wonderful Day 47
A Chilly Night 48
Nature 48
Looking Around 49
Soulmate 49
A Long Night 50
A Trip to Church 50
Thinking of You 51
A Celebration 51
Mr. Dishy 52
A Precious Bud 52
Miss Wonderful 53
My World 53
My Dream 54
Miss Perfect 54
Juicy Tomatoes 55
Sad Old Dog 55
Remembering 56
Dearest Friend 56
Interests 57
I Wonder 57
The North Star 58
Guiding Star 58
Deep Sleep 58
Precious Little Darling 59
Early-Morning Call 59
Sweetest Little Bundle 59
My Little Darling 60
To the One I Love the Most 60
Mystery Man 61
Unhappy 61
Friend 62
Our Gran 62
Feelings 63
Lucy 63
The Joining of Hands 64
True Friends 64
The Beach 65
A New Generation 65
Little Sunshine 66
Thinking 66
Little Puss 67
Little Old Steam Engine 67
My Little Tam 68
Sweet Little Man 68
Shining Bright 69
Thoughts of Yesterday 69
A Cold Night 70
Baby 70
My Man 71
A Séance 71
Old Blue Eyes 72
Shock Horror 72
Sweet Little Boy 73
You 73
Mischief Maker 74
Asking for Forgiveness 74

What a Night 75
Beautiful Girl 75
A Night to Remember 76
My Angel 76
Our Vows 77
On the Dance Floor 77
Out in the Cold 78
My Cat 78
A Fresh Frosty Day 79
The Tale of a Christmas Tree 79
Bath Time 80
Being There 80
A Jolly Christmas 81
The Gathering 81
To Reflect 82
Waiting for Santa 82
Melting Ice 83
Snoozing 83
Having a Party 84
Flying Around the World 84
Loving You 85
Adorable 85
A Joyous Day 86
Mum 86
What's Going On 87
Clever Girl 87
A Noisy Night 88
Junior 88
A New Dawn 89
The Trio 89
Relaxation 90
Us 90
A New Day 91
My Baby 91
Time to Go 92
A Friend so True 92
Pests 93
Mates 93
My Lover 94
Miserable Dog 94
Young at Heart 95
The Universe 95
Lou Lou 96
Sleep Walking 96
Happy Dog 97
Relaxation 97
Us 98
Kids 98
Playing a Match 99
The Resurrection 99
My Hubby 100
My Darling 100
Thinking On 101
Being Dazzled 101
Ringo 102
A Mad Pooch 102
One Night 103
Little Monkey 103
The Dead of Night 104
A Meeting 104
My Puss 105
Tammy 105
My Son in Law 106
A New Baby 106
A Gliding Plane 107
A Party 107
My Man Ray 108

A Jolly Poem 108
An Eternal Love 109
A Cheerful Poem 109
A Trickster 110
The Visitor 110
A Crying Baby 111
A Silent Night 111
Another Day 112
A Busy Day 112
Family Prayer 113
My Boy 113
A Beautiful Day 114
You Will Always Be My Rock 114
Little Angels 115
Having Fun 115
Looking On 116
Sizzling with Delight 116
Leaving a Parcel 117
Buddies 117
Butterflies 118
The Final Days 118
Darling Daughter 119
Artful Dodger 120
Being Together 120
One So Precious 121
My Lovable Yorkie 121
A Quiet Moment 122
Christmas Day 122
Little Tubby Chops 123
My Precious, Precious Baby 123
A Sweet Little Lady 124
The Colors of a Rainbow 124
A Scrap 125
Hunted 125
The Fattest Pig in Town 126
In Festive Spirit 127
Little Miss Artful 127
Queen of Cats 128
Getting Ready 128
Up to Trouble 129
My Ginger Tom 129
A Doggie Crowned 130
King of the Cats 130
A Day to Remember 131
Thoughts of Today 131
Swimming Gracefully 132
The Joining Together 132
Homeward Bound 133
Going to a Party 133
Jumping Out 134
The Unwrapping of Presents 134
A Windy Day 135
Going on Her Travels 135
Down in the Dumps 136
Another Year to Remember 136
Tam the Greatest 137
My Other Half 138
Start of a New Year 138
Said in a Heated Moment 139
A Daft Fellow 139
My Mother-in-Law 140

So He Lives to See Another Day 140
Trusting God 141
At War 141
Prince of All Pussy Cats 142
End of the Road 142
Reckless 143
Chances 143
It Is So You 144
My Little Tufty 144
One of the Best 145
Two Great Friends 145
Mr. Tittle Mouse 146
A Blustery Day 146
A Charmer 147
A Doggy Tale 147
On a Date 148
Remembering the Times 148
Keeping up the Beat 149
Wishing You Were Here 149
Out and About 150
Great Nan 150
Two Brothers 151
Shower Time 151
Time to Wind Down 152
Playing Football 152
A Crazy Night 153
A Letter to a Valentine 153
Dedication in Verse 154
My Darling Yorkie 154
Losing My Temper 155
A Chocoholic 155
A Proposal 156
Mummy's Little Baby 156
Missing You 157
My Big Brother 157
I So Happy 158
My Darling 158
A Dog up to Mischief 159
Fondly Remembered 159
Grandfather 160
A Little Cherub 160
Roli 161

Love of My Life

Tonight's the night, my darling
Tonight's the night, my love
Although I hear you
You're always in my heart
Oh, my darling, you hear me
Up in the skies above
Forever in my heart, sweetheart
Forever in my heart, my love.

Faithful Friend

Two big brown eyes looking up at you
With love in their heart
Faithful through and through
The fur is brown tinged
With ginger and black
A loveable rogue
From front to back
This is how I see him like this
A faithful hound not to be missed.

Wedding Day

Hark the wedding bells are ringing
For this Joyous Day:
To celebrate ones coming together
On this Wonderful Way
The bride and groom in Matrimony
Singing to the Savior
We clap hands together in harmony
To be bonded together forever.

Baby Girl

With pointy ears
And a pricked up nose
This is my cat wherever she goes
With white soft fur
And a gleaming coat
With claws full out
Ready to pounce
She moves her legs
From side to side
This graceful creature
With the big green eyes.

Hurry Scurry

Mousey, mousey
Don't be slow
Mousey, mousey
Quick as you go
Scurry, scurry
Throughout the night
Don't be giving us a fright
On an on you run and flee
Give us time to get the tea.

Rockabye Baby

Night-night, baby
Night-night
Sleep tight, baby
Sleep tight
Cry all your might
Someone will hear you
Don't take a fright
Hush, little baby, go to sleep
Mama's coming by, so don't you weep.

Dear Friend

My little poochy-woochy Pumpkin chops
My little smooch-woo
You're always with me
Wherever I go
The friend so dear to me
You're the sweetest thing I know
My little poochy-woochy Pumpkin chops
My little smoochy-woo.

A Special Friendship

My precious, precious baby
The one I understand
She is always around me
Whenever I'm at hand
She is such a little treasure
A darling to know
I know who to come home to
So there's no contest you know
She lies down beside me
A mad dog for all to see
Wouldn't be without her
She's the greatest girl for me.

Runaway Train

Choo-choo
Chug-chug
Blowing the horn
Puffing away
On a Sunday morn'
Round and round the
Bend she goes
Where to nobody knows
Wheels wind round
Going past
This old engine is going fast.

Mouse on the Go

Mousey, mousey
Go and get lost
Your game's up
I'm the boss
With teeth turned out
And raring to go
Your squeak so loud
The cat will show
Wonder what's around the corner now
If you're not careful, you'll give out a wail
Your fur is brown
And Whiskas long
With claws so sharp
And a tail so strong.

Trusted Friend

Yorkie, Yorkie
Curley as can be
You're the one
Lovely for me
You cuddle away
To my dismay
With all barrels loaded
Fat and bloated
You lick away
To your heart's content
The look on your face
Is all that's meant
The love of my life is you
Forever more it's true.

The King

Fluff ball
Tuff ball
Fluffy little tufty
Handsome cat
In the world
All fat and scruffy
Is my little tufty
Beautiful as told
Little ginger
Tail bent
He's the prowler
With a scent.

Game's Up

Pitter-patter
If you dare
Hurry-scurry
If you care
Mousey, mousey
Got to run
Today's the day
You're having fun
Pussy on the warpath now
Time's up, so hurry
You're too late to scurry
The traps are set
Your maker is met
All is quiet
Not a mouse in the house.

Little Baby

With blue eyes peering up at me
Eyes so small, barely can see
With skin so soft
And a tender touch
This little person is loved very much
To this little fellow, life is unreal
His mum's leaning forward
It's time for a meal.

Having a Tough Day

My dog's a pickle
Don't she just know it
She lays there all quiet
And tends not to show it
With tongue hanging out
She lets off steam
All the time this goes on
She having a dream
She lays back
Has her say
In all this
What a day.

My Prince Charming

With eyes of blue
And a smile so inviting
You're the prince for which
I'm waiting
With curly brown hair
Near to dark black as can be
You're the soul especially for me
Quite a kisser so you are
Haven't forgotten the way
We were
All fed up and nowhere to go
You're quite a catch and don't we know
Miss you so very much
Hardly seems long since we were in touch
Your smiley face and a look so precious
Can't help think of us being adventurous.

Achieving Something

Things of today gone tomorrow
Always remembered forever in sorrow
With life that's gone by
We can only try
Life's a mountain we have to climb
To get to the top, is that a crime?
Taking one step at a time.

Worshipping You

Far away up in the sky above
Is the man that I love
Looking down on us night and day
Guarding us come what may
Eyes looking up with warmth and love
A meaning for the word dove
With the gentleness in his eyes
It's hard to say our goodbyes.

Little Treasure

With eyes of brown and a bonny little face
My girl Tam is a big ace
Smothered with love and soft as butter
She can hardly utter
She is like the cat that got the cream
And to her it's a dream
She's a loveliest pooch
Who don't give a hooch.

My Lover

My darling
Wherever you are
You will always be my shining star
Sparkling all night
Forever bright
Scattered one by one
Stars each and every one
As you shine down on me
I will remember the
Good and bad times we had
Still think I instead
The love we shared shows we cared.

Little Star

Pretty girl staring up at me
Eyes full of love for all to see
Charming first thing in the morning
Up with the lark when it's dawning
We take life together in every way
Sometimes we just can't get out of the hay
So loyal, trusting and true
Is my tammy boo
Always glad to have to her around
She keeps me on solid ground.

Remembering You

Up in the sky
The clouds go bye
Thinking of you with twinkle in my eye
Heaven around
Good to the touch
Always remembered
I love you very much
Blue above
The sign of love
Thoughts of you
Make me be true
When my days have ended
And the going is rough
Life has been tough
All will be lost
You and I together
Forever and ever
Our spirits joined
Never to be parted
Sleep tight, sweetheart.

A Drama Queen

With eyes of love
And a look so gleaming
My young mutt's so appealing
With brown beady eyes
And a wet black nose
She has gone for a doze
Laying there for all to see
She is the smartest one, don't you agree.

Loving You

You are my sunshine
You are my love
You are in the skies above
Thinking of you night and day
This does not go away
With a heart of gold
Afraid to grow old
You've always been there
I've done as I'm told
Missing you badly
Loving you gladly
You're the sweetest and light
You're my delight
Forever in my thoughts.

Beautiful Rose

Wild, wild rose
As red as can be
Beauty all around
For everyone to see
Growing tall
Sharp as can be
Fading in color
For you and me
The smell is divine
And a scent so sickly
This plant can often be prickly.

In Our Thoughts

With eyes so precious
And a love so strong
You're the meek and wonderful one
You follow me with paws of wonder
It's great to see you not going under
Missed so much, it's hard to say
Wonder how you got away
You and I got together
It will always be forever and ever
What I will do without you
No one will ever know
Looking up at the skies
That surround you
You sparkle and you glow.

Piggy Porker

Wrinkled brown as a little pumpkin
My girl's a little dumpling
She's so sweet
I can tweet
Doing the business with her feet
Always around
So I found
She's my lovable friend
Trusting and true
Always there when I feel blue
With big brown pointy ears
Picks up noise to a treat
Always hungry, loves her meat.

A Tribute

To you, my pet
Wherever you are
For you have been there forever more
No matter how much you cost
You I have loved the most
To me, you were dear
Life ended too soon, I fear
Counting the days you are not here
Miss you so much
I can hardly bear
Thoughts of what happen
Touch me to the core
Life's not the same
You're not here anymore.

Tammy

You're a licker
You're a flicker
You're a fidgety fan
Always on the go
Whenever you can
You're my darling
You're my baby
You're my sweet little lady
Clean as you go
You are very slow
You drawl at the lips
You lick your chops
You're the one to look at the box
Sweet as a nut you are
You're a diamond
You are a star.

Going a Distance

Up and away in the cloud so high
A balloon on a wave of air goes by
Miles and miles it does go
Where to, goodness knows
Traveling in the sky at speed
Making up for charity and need
Wonder where it's landing now
Germany or Switzerland somehow
Birds fly high and peer down
This little balloon's on high ground.

Letting Off Steam

Scritch-scratch
Love you very much
Snifflley-difflley, you're very prickly
Dam-dam, you're my man
Forever true
You're always blue
In the skies above
You're always my love
Sweetness and light, you're my delight
You're always loving and giving
Working for a living
From now to the end
I will understand.

Being Happy

You are the laughter
You are my life
The hours we spent together
Every day of our lives
The things we remember
Through thick and thin
This has been since life began
The tears in the morning
The kisses in the night
This was surely my delight
Thought of night and day
What would a girl say.

My Grandson

Blonde-blonde
Little boy
You bring me such a lot of joy
Into everything you are
You are my guiding star
A lot of love you bring
Makes me want to sing
Having you around
Is positively sound
Love you lots
You're always playing with the pots
A little minx you are
You had a ride in the car
We have lots of fun
Me and you and Mum.

The Terrors

Two cats sitting on the mat
One looks up and that is that
Out comes a third up
To mischief and playing around
This I finally found
While I was wondering about
What the devil's on the ground, I shout
Using paws to get a ball on the floor
Tossing and turning
And out through the door.

Bonfire Night

Logs on the fire
Children about
No time to worry or shout
Today's the day, it's sizzling time
Sausages on the go
It's got to be nine
Buns in the oven doing fine
Wonder how many will be mine
Flashes appearing outside
Sparklers glowing in numbers
To our wonder
A beautiful sight
You might get a fright
Guy sitting curled on top
Any minute now, the sparks will pop
A bonfire in all its glory
Around to tell the story.

Dear Grandad

Grandad's a star
High up and far
Looking down on me
With absolute glee
Smiling in awe
As I go to school
Proud as punch
I love him so much
Miss him smoking
Never, ever joking
Telly addict
Always getting a packet
Wish he was here
He always got a beer
Puffing away
What can I say.

Up to Tricks

Dozy-dozy
Pussy's all cozy
Snug as a bug
Fit for a rug
Scruffy and fluffy
Is king tufty
Ears pricked up
Ready to jump
Already for a scrap
Got himself in a flap.

Always You

A long time ago
Before I knew you
I traveled about as you do
Life was good
Life was precious
Something happened that day
To change my way
Meeting you and everything you are
Loving you
You are my star
Missed so much
You're one of a bunch
Picked till it's tender
Love you very much.

Lord

Twinkle, twinkle
Little star
You are the greatest
You are, you are
Up in the sky
Miles so high
You are to me one hell of
A kind of guy
People worship you by far
You are the guiding star
You teach us all we know
Showing us the way to go
Bright light shining down
Glaring causing us to frown
Everyone watching from all around
Snowflakes falling on the ground.

Christmas Day

Hey-ho, it's Christmas on the go
Hurry up now, you don't want to be slow
Festive food and things galore
This is not the time to snore
Up in bed he creeps about
Keep quiet now and don't shout
Whisper all you can
Santa won't be coming again
Decorations put up one by one
Keep going now till it's done
All's well and we're having fun
Christmas has just begun.

Mr. Loveable

Dandy the great
Was in a crate
Big cat of all time
Who was only nine
Soft to the touch
Loved brushing very much
He had a friend
Whom he loved to the end
She was only seven
When she went to heaven
He missed her very much
And her magical touch
Sad not to have her around
It is true she was a pal he found.

All United

The candle flickers till the
Wind is no more
All lit-up lanterns galore
The start of service where people gather
The church stands tall in the weather
Impressive so it is
Has us spellbound like this
All is quiet
Not even a word
Prayers are spoken
We're not even heard
Singing all together
Music playing as if forever.

A Sweetheart

Little baby up in arms
Got his mother's little charms
Sound asleep
So quiet, not a peep
Beautiful baby asleep
With sweet angelic looks
Bonny too
He's so chubby just like you.

Night Before Christmas

The lights that are bright
And sparkle in the night
Christmas comes early
Everyone's in bed
Shops stacked full
Ready for the call
Children everywhere and in sight
Decorations going up
With all their might
Music playing all around
Making a very loud sound
Santa roaming somewhere
Children from the night air
Rain splattering down
Makes me want to frown.

A Day of Fishing

Spats the cat
Went out one day
Catching fish in the pond to play
Jumping in to take a swim
This of course made him grim
Round and round they did go
The cat of course was very slow
Aware of what was going on
The fish dived down, then they were gone.

The Wonder of the World

Counting stars
One, two, three
Looking down
For us to see
Bright and beautiful
Shine do thee
These little stars
White as can be
Far up high
Twinkle in the sky
Symbol of the Lord
As years go by.

The Festivities Have Begun

Wishes for Christmas
And the New Year
The chinking of glasses
To bring us good cheer
Well-wishers all way around
Picking presents that they have found
Father Christmas is due here
Wonder what he's bringing this year.

A Busy Santa

Here comes Santa
Down memories lane
With toys on his back
Enough to fill a sack
Things will not be the same
Every little boy and girl
Will have a game or gift
Dancing around a snowman
Santa giving a lift
Oh, Mr. Santa, you have come to tea
What a nice surprise for me.

Little Princess

Sweet little foxy face
My little treasure
You're everything to me
With ears pricked back
Alert in every way
She's the girl for me
Wags her tail and with all her might
Lays on her back and think she's alright
Apart from all this
A great little miss
The best in the world.

A Big Sleep

Fluffy and curly as can be
I'm in bed as you can see
Curled up tight in a ball
Ears alert and that's not all
The heat's on and I'm all warm
Now I am ready for a big yawn.

Mouse Hunter

Here I am, lord of the house
I can't catch anything
Not even a mouse
I sit and purr all day long
The mistress wakes us all
Up with a very loud gong
When they all come home
They come to greet me
Getting things ready till
It's time for tea.

Bonfire Frenzy

Pitter-patter
Spit and splatter
Logs crackling on the fire
The spit sizzling turning around
Looking tasty as we found
People chatting all day long
Gathering together for a midnight song
Tables full with food galore
This is not a bore
Fireworks blazing
Which is amazing
Lighting up the sky
Music playing loud as can be
This is certainly enough for me.

A Day of It

Pitter-patter
What's the matter
Down comes the rain
What a pain
Up with the lark
In the dark
Nothing will be the same
It's been a terrible game
Playing together after all these years
Bringing back all the fears
Now we're home
We quite agree
Now it's time for tea.

Fighting the Enemy

Rolling around with her legs in the air
Waving about without a care
Touch her if you dare
With eyes gazing
And ears pricked back
She knows she's under attack
This little cat with the green eyes
Spitting and spatting to our surprise
With claws curled out
And ready to pounce
If that's not all
Scrapping away to their dismay
A fight under way.

Hay-Ho for Santa

Clap hands
Here we go again
Time for Santa
And his parcels galore
This is what we all adore
Reindeer standing
Antlers arched
All set and ready for a march
Santa waiting
Time to fly
Kids want to cry
Everyone merry for a special day
This is good in every way.

Little Angel

My grandson has got toys galore
Which he adores
Some big, some small
Although he's not very tall
He's one very lucky little boy
And a great big joy
He smiles a lot
When he gets the pot
He's so full of fun
He loves his bun
An angel he is
Which I will miss
Love very much
Shall keep in touch
When they go away
I would like to say:
"I will help you on your way
Baby can have a play."

Time to Go

Time flies
It is now goodbye
Sometimes it makes me cry
Seeing baby, I want to laugh
I don't know, maybe I'm daft
We're up all day with things to say
I wonder how we got away
I have enjoyed my stay very much
Even when my grandson and me touched
He's the cutest one in the world
I would miss him if it were told
He's a lovable, huggable boy
And a very big joy.

A Restless Tot

You're always in trouble
Come to me at the double
You're a tinker, that you are
You're a stinker by far
Loved a lot
I'll smack your bot
Cheeky as can be
Come on now, I'll give you some tea
Your dad's about
He may want to shout.

Miss Charming

A show of teeth
Pearly whites
To her delight
My dog gives a fright
With her gnashers ready
Have to keep her steady
A smile in the morning
Which comes without warning
Lovely to see
Don't you agree
All brown and curly
Gets up early
One of the best
Daft like the rest
What a smasher
Quite a cracker.

A Believer

Holy-holy
My God, I am only
A sinner to this day
Forever do I pray
Things that go wrong
I must be strong
Everything out in the open
The Bible is a token
For beliefs that come my way
This I have to pay
To thee I worship
Making so many friendships
As I go about it alone
Come what may.

A Special Day

A candle blowing in the wind
A bird flying as if sinned
Two doves cooing
Not a sound or a word
Forever in mind unheard
The coming of peace
Forever will cease
We gather together
In the stormy weather
His name forever more
As we open the door
The whole world in mind
Are we being kind
To this day in a way
We will do it, come what may.

Joy

Hip-hip, hooray
A baby's on the way
Now we can start
Preparing for the part
It will be life-changing
And will need rearranging
A girl or a boy
Hard to say
Whatever it will be
It will be a joy
Company for the boy
I'm so glad to say
I'm happy to this day
Let the bells ring out
So we can all shout.

Dreaming of a Peaceful Day

With joys of spring
Let us begin
A blue sky above
There flies a dove
The sign of peace
Will the noises ever cease
Quiet as can be
Would be nice for you and me.

June

A time to remember
Time to have fun
This is the time when we'd all begun
Holding hands for all to see
This is the time for you and me
Slowly changing day by day
Making life good in every way.

A Happy Day

Digging up daises
All of a flutter
This is why I think I'm a nutter
A blue sky above
Spring is on its way
Birds singing
Hip-hip, hooray
A smile first thing in the morning
Having a cry at night
A good combination and a delight.

Thinking Back

Blue is the color
My feeling of now
In deep gloom do I feel
Is this possibly real
The sun is gone and the day is grey
Up comes the morning
Without any warning
Rain pouring down
Causing me to frown
Miserable it's been
Wish I was a teen.

Keeping Together

Tossing and turning
Unable to see
Warm and comfortable
Curling up to thee
This is how life should be
You and me, together are we
As the years went on, we were mad
There were also times that we were sad
Breaking up would be hard, we know
Maybe one day, it will be time to go.

My Girl

Sneaky-peaky
My girl is always stinky
With eyes that look up
She is ready to shut up
Love is in the air
She sits and stares to my despair
She makes me cry
I wonder why
We have been together so long
Getting to know someone else would be wrong
We are together for keeps
Forgetting about all those weeps.

The Time of Your Life

Pussycat, pussycat
Where have you been
You're like the puss who got the cream
Licking your Whiskas
With all your might
You of course look a fright
Your mistress is around
And going up the wall
If she's not careful
She will have a fall
Pussycat, pussycat
Wonder what's for tea
Kippers or monkfish for you and me
Living together, you purr all the time
Wonder when the clock strikes nine.

Naughty Puppy

Tiddles the puppy
Was all sad and bad
He hid in the corner
As if he were mad
Poor little thing
Out one day
Trod on something hard
Bent down to lay
His mistress came over
He had to obey
This little puppy was afraid all day
He met other dogs on the way
Waited until he was called
Wondering what his mistress would say.

A Wonderful Day

The joy of spring is here
To bring us good cheer
The birds singing loudly so we can hear
Time to sit down and have a beer
Nature's important for the wonders of the earth
I often think about what it's worth
The flowers are out and in bloom
While the world is in the shadows of gloom
Every day something is read
I end up taking it home to bed
Life is one jumble and don't we know it
Just one tumble and we've blown it.

A Chilly Night

Twilight moonlight
Owls come out at night
Pecking away to our dismay
Hooting all their might
From dark till light
An eeriness in the air
I of course don't care
Chilly it has become
This is not welcome
With hands cold as ice
This is not very nice.

Nature

Rain or sunshine
Come what may
This is a season
So what do we say
Bad weather or good weather is what we get
Hot or cold with the seasons yet
The years go by as we go living
Time ticks fast as we go on giving.

Looking Around

Rosie, Rosie
Forever cozy
Cuddled up to your heart's content
After a long time having spent
Up and down the streets of town
Looking for a bus
What a clown
London's packed, so you can see
Crowds all around
I want to flee
The big wheel, a view from the top
If I'm not careful, it may not stop.

Soulmate

Honey, honey
You're my one and only
Today, tomorrow, and forever
Until we're all lonely
You're my angel
You're my wife
You're the good thing in my life
Mother to my children
Loving and true
You're always here
When I am blue
Missus, so much I go under
Whenever you're not around, I make a blunder.

A Long Night

Cold and eerie
Black and dismal
Wind blowing
Night-time glowing
Candle flickering through
Passed from me to you
Shiver, shiver
Chatter, chatter
Wonder when we can have a natter
Up in the morning
On a Sunday dawn
Birds sing out for us to morn
Off to church do us go
Me and Mum and a lot of snow
Quiet all around
Not even a sound.

A Trip to Church

Twisting and turning
Forever yearning
Thoughts of yesterday
Memories that drift away
Time heals fast
Although we're in the past
A message from heaven
While we're staying in Devon
The church beacons us to it
As we enter God's door
Music sounds out forever more
A powerful feeling flows through us
After which, we catch a bus.

Thinking of You

For the man that you are
You drive me too far
Up every morning
Without any warning
Don't get any sleep
Even when I'm counting sheep
To this very day
In the month of May
I remember you
You're the one that I love
In my heart and above
Forever missing you
Can this be honestly true
You're my one and only
And I feel blue.

A Celebration

Jumping up with joy
I shout out and cry
An air all around
Today I found
A happiness so strong
Can that be wrong
Must spread the news
Family first
Have a great thirst
Out pops the bubbly
Taking care not to be wobbly
A party to arrange
Even though it is strange.

Mr. Dishy

Fabulous in a round
About sort of way
You're the must-have of the day
Looking about for something to wear
I must of course declare
You're the dish of the day
And I love you in a great way
Happy of course I am
Hope you feel like the big man you deserve to be
You're wonderful, as you can see.

A Precious Bud

The flower that blooms
Is beautiful as can be
A precious soul for you and me
Its tender buds all bright and perky
The leaves all silky and smooth
Laying in a groove
Blowing in the wind forever more
And for to grow it
Need the rain to pour
Getting stronger and taller as it flaps about
And another bloom opens
Up and it pops out.

Miss Wonderful

You're my sweetness
You're my gem
You're the one thing that's part of them
Always on lookout
Every now and then
Don't know how to give up now and when
Always on duty
Never off
Ready to bark
Always getting told off
You're my treasure
You're quite a girl
You're the one who
Could give a twirl.

My World

Lover with the brown curly hair
You bring me everything, even cheer
With long bushy eyebrows
Grey beard to match
I would love to have been your catch
You sit there with misery in your eyes
I wonder if you would
Rather have a disguise
You're like a shrinking violet
Wouldn't say boo to a goose
I sometimes think you would rather have a
noose
A day's too much for you to boast.

My Dream

You're my baby
You're my dear
You're the one
I like quite near
You're my sweetheart
You're the best
You're even better than the rest
You're my lover
You're my best friend
I will love you till the end.

Miss Perfect

Kitty, kitty
You sit there pretty
You sparkle and shine
You are divine
You sit there alert
Having been on the dirt
Wonder how you were ever mine
Little you are
Crafty by far.

Juicy Tomatoes

Tiny, forever small
You're the pick of them all
Whatever you are
You're one of the best
Try to sort you out
You're better than the rest
Rosy-red, succulent and moist
Takes time to chew but very nice.

Sad Old Dog

Dandy, bandy
The three-legged dog
Hoping on one leg
Like an old sod
Struggled to get around
Sometimes he didn't care
Everywhere he went
They had to beware
Got in the way he did
Brave that he was
He was at a loss
Nobody knew quite what it cost.

Remembering

Roses are red
Violet are blue
You'll always be my lover
And I will have you
We will always be there for each other
Since life'd begun
For you and I had a lot of fun
Missed so much
Day to day
There was always something to say.

Dearest Friend

You're my friend
So dear to me
Come what may
This is what you mean to me
We're so close
We are one
This is how we began
You a pup, me an owner
Taking our time out
No longer a loner
You're my baby
You drive me crazy
But one thing I know
I will never let you go
You mean so much to me
We belong together, as you can see
For now, this is how it will be.

Interests

Wonders of art
Creativity it makes
Landscapes galore
Which I adore
Out in the fields
Miles and miles
The beauty to paint
Which is quaint
To be adventurous
And discover more
Life is precious
It can also be a bore.

I Wonder

I wonder here
I wonder there
I wonder everywhere
I sit alone and sit and stare
Wondering where I go from there
Up in the morning
Thinking of the day
Wondering how it will go my way.

The North Star

You're my guiding star
You're the shiniest by far
You twinkle through the night
To my delight
You're miles and miles away
You sparkle for all to see
In all your glory
You could tell a story
A heavenly star you are
Drifting towards another star.

Guiding Star

Granddad looking down from afar
You're the one that we adore
Sadly missed along the way
There are things we wanted to say
Thought of every day
Only time will tell
We are doing well
The years go by
And we ask ourselves why.

Deep Sleep

Sleeping heavily, I say
Is something that can happen every day
Dreaming so much, it's hard to stop
The things you imagine
Jumbled up till we pop.

Precious Little Darling

A little darling that you are
You have been sent from afar
A blessing to your mum and dad
No time to think of being sad
Thought about for so long
Every day you get strong
A little mite that you are
You're a little wonderful star.

Early-Morning Call

I heard a cuckoo call
In the month of May
It was early in the morning dew
I didn't want it to go away
How beautiful it sounded
I couldn't believe my luck
It took me by surprise
I nearly ended up in muck.

Sweetest Little Bundle

Hush a bye, sweetheart
Hush a bye now
You're God's gift from heaven
You're cute, you're sweet
You give everyone a treat
You're mummy and daddy's little soldier
Making waves for your big brother
A little bundle that you are
Loved so much, you're a very tiny star.

My Little Darling

You lay there looking lost
Tongue hanging out
Shattered at a cost
No woes or cares
Now and then stares
All worn to a frazzle
Coat need clipping
Tired by living
What a life you lead
You like it best
When you are freed
A pooch's life you have
The best that you can get
A mate you have not met.

To the One I Love the Most

To you, my darling, way up high
You're my one and only guy
Special to the end
You will always be my friend
Thought of and loved the most
I will cherish you
When I think of you
I feel blue
Remembering all your different ways
The thing you did all the days
Long-time forgotten you will never be
Because you will always belong to me
You will always be a part of me
That is a promise, you will always be true.

Mystery Man

Loving you with all my might
You are the guy on the right
Tall, dark, handsome to boot
You're always the one with the loot
Always sharing, very, very proud
You're always having
Your radio on loud
Creating noise within the street
Policemen are on the beat
The joys of you when we meet
Then we have to find a good seat.

Unhappy

Laying there silent and forlorn
Looking sorry as though you don't belong
You look at me with those black eyes
A look of sadness meets my eyes
You talk to me with sheer pain
I am wondering what we gained
I love you so much, it hurts.

Friend

A friend is genuine
A friend is good
A friend is there
When you're in a mood
She is there every day
With a care, come what may
Know them for years
Always there when you're in tears
A friend stands by you
Even if you are blue
A friend so dear to you never strays
Just stays home and prays.

Our Gran

A gran is a dedicated lady
Who is warm and generous
She cares for her family tirelessly
Through the years, she takes the strain
Minding the children and more to her name
She is loving and true
And picks you up when you are blue
She is lovely
Her knowledge is positively sound
And what we have found
She's the greatest person to have around.

Feelings

Loving you is easy
It's hard for me to say
Loving you brings brighter things each day
You cheered me up, no end
I am glad that you were my friend
Losing you broke my heart
It eventually tore me apart
Now counting days to
The anniversary of your parting
Celebrated every year
Since you're gone, I fear
If only you knew how I felt
Your heart would melt.

Lucy

There you are, lying snug as a bug in a rug
Curled up all content as can be
One of a three
You're lovely to me
Not a care
Must beware
The cutest cat of all
Even though you're small
You dream like us all.

The Joining of Hands

Two rings joined together
With words forever
In harmony so they say
Living day to day
Eternity in every way
Life is a mountain
A long way to climb
As long as you are together
Life will be fine
Worlds apart from the very start
Two loves joined together, never to part.

True Friends

Jump up and down
Look around and see
Friends for you and friends for me
All smiling happy as can be
Going through life like you and me
Peace you need and calm too
Without this, it makes you blue.

The Beach

Hi-ho, hi-ho
The waves come over me
Hi-ho, hi-ho, down by the sea
Shining, shining bright
The moon, a big ball at night
The sand hot to your feet
Scalding continually
Till we meet
Peace and quiet
The day has begun
Now's the time to have fun.

A New Generation

We watch them grow
From little to tall
From fat to thin
Which says it all
Our children, wise from years with us
Tomorrow's the word or we'll go bust
As years take their toll
Our children grow old
With sense behind them
They have been told
Time is short, they have to hold
No longer do we have our children at heart
Others do take as we have to part.

Little Sunshine

Good morning, little girl
You're the sweetest of my dreams
You've always been there it seems
One minute I'm lonely, forever only
Now we're together
Forever and ever
As long as you're around
I have finally found
A dog so true and loyal
You're the one thing I spoil
A darling to me
I will remember thee.

Thinking

In a dream I am
Wonder what I will face if I can
In a dream I am hopeful
On a mountain I will tumble
Landing so hard, I stumble
A rumble from below
A splatting of tiny snow
Cold as ice
Not very nice
Don't think twice.

Little Puss

Kitty, kitty
Sweet, sweet kitty
You're the sweetest in the world
You sit and purr
Smothered in fur
Cleaning as you go
Going very slow
You stroll around on all fours
Walking through all the doors
With not a care
Will you dare
To stroll out once more.

Little Old Steam Engine

Wheels wind around going past
This old engine is going fast
Puffing merrily all day long
Jumping on to sing a song
We're all going to blow the horn
Merrily as we go along
Past all fields and meadows
Where she goes, nobody knows.

My Little Tam

There goes a bark
A cry that is clear
I wipe my eyes
To have you near
Thoughts of every day
Thoughts of today
Keeps me wondering in every way
To have and to hold
To me you were really bold
You were the master in every disaster.

Sweet Little Man

With a cross-eyed look
My cat looks like hook
With a black eye, he's all
Covered up and shy
A handsome cat
All proud and fat
All white with big black spots
Waddles along as he trots
From side to side he goes
Walking on tiptoes
Loves a fight with all his might
Picks on others to his delight
That's old Ringo alright.

Bright

ıy man
ıf we can

uide
d forever true

ue
rld
u are
e myself, now you're a star.

Thoughts of Yesterday

Forgive me, my dear
Although you are not here
A long time has passed
Since we last got together
Thought of in many ways
Sorry for things that have gone wrong
Back in those days
You were my rock, so it seems
Cannot do without you, even in my dreams.

A Cold Night

Rain, come shine
Here's to the wine
Dew in the morning
Red sky without warning
First rain of the season
Comes without reason
Midnight upon us
All dark and dreamy
So very, very scary
The night owl gives a hoot
Candle lit and flickering
A wind blowing outside
Doors creaking
Squeaking up the stairs
Mugs of cocoa brewing
Steaming hot from the pot
To warm us up whether
We like it or not.

Baby

Little one, little one
Your life has not begun, growing so contently
Although you're not even one
Only just thought of
Wanted very much
You're the one thing they wished for
So they can feel your touch
Your granddad's looking down at you
Now and forever more
You will be someone who we can adore.

My Man

I touch your head
I ruffle your hair
Curly and wavy
Cut with flair
With blue eyes
And long eyelashes
You come and go in flashes
A very bristly beard
As grey as can be
A rugged sort of face
Just for me
The love we had for each other
Does not go away
Thinking of you day to day.

A Séance

The night is young
Eerie is theory
Spooky till the end
When we need a friend
Dark, so dark
Drizzly all night
Noise of creaking
Causing a fright
Doors banging
Cats meowing
Dogs howling
Through the night.

Old Blue Eyes

I look at you
You look at me
With eyes of love
Which was not to be
Taken too soon
For no reason to me
My heart's not in it
As you can see
With the bluest of eyes
And the wisest of the lot
You are who I got
Thought of so dearly
Remembering so clearly
A man of my dreams for so long
Always and forever more
You I always adore.

Shock Horror

With piercing blue eyes
You take me by surprise
With long eyelashes that flicker
You're a nose-picker
A love for you
Makes me blue
With big ears that point out
You're a freak, there's no doubt
Love so much
Miss the way we touched
The cuddles and the smoochy kisses
It's bye-bye to the missus.

Sweet Little Boy

Little one, little one
You're the sweetest of them all
Small and tiny
And not very big at all
With little fingers and little toes
And a cute little nose
You lay there like an angel
All warm and snug
The loveliest one on the rug.

You

With a grin on your face
And a smug look
You'll be the one first in my book
You sit there proud as can be
Looking adoringly at me
You're the handsomest one I know
You are always on the go.

Mischief Maker

Squiggle-giggle, I'm a little pickle
With fair skin
And a sweet little grin
I don't know where you've just been
Into cupboards and the lock
You've always got
Your mind on the shoes
Toys picked up and thrown everywhere
What a mess I do declare
You're a little urchin
We had better beware.

Asking for Forgiveness

I say my prayers to you Lord above
You are indeed who I love
I get up in the day
So what can I say
I visit you from time to time
Your church stands tall
Although I'm small
Your stained glass windows
Stand out for thee
I of course must go home for tea.

What a Night

What's this a game
It's a real shame
Didn't get started
Because we parted
Turned the lights out
The cat's about
Scrambling around
Going nuts, so I found
All quiet now
Sure is hell
Do not know what to do
I feel blue
What's going on
Feel like making a song to cheer me along.

Beautiful Girl

Long, tall
Little or small
You are weeny
And I am a beany
As things go, you are a teeny
Growing all the time
Soon you will be nine
With blonde beautiful hair
And a look so rare
This I cannot compare
You are the sweetest thing on earth
I adore you for what it's worth
You have me in stitches
You're cheeky to boot
Love you very much.

A Night to Remember

Dance, my darling
Dance all night
You're with me and that's alright
We snuggle up
To our delight
Smooch about
Don't want to cause a fright
The music soft
And playing well
This is swell
Time's up, the dance has ended
Gone are the people we befriended
Time to go home
We're all alone.

My Angel

You're always in trouble
Come to me at the double
You're a tinker, that you are
You're a stinker by far
Loved a lot
I'll smack your bot
Cheeky as can be
Come on now, I'll give you some tea.

Our Vows

Torn apart
We're poles apart
Forever forlorn
Until the dawn
Forever in my heart
We will never part
You are the one
Till this day and the rest
For better, for worse
Richer and poorer
In sickness and in health
I will be there.

On the Dance Floor

Hip-hip, hooray
Swinging time I say
Waggling those hips
As we do our flips
On crowded floor
We can do no more
Jigging and dancing around
Avoiding falling on the ground
A lot of noise all around
Hardly making a sound
Jumping and banging about
Feel like I want to shout.

Out in the Cold

Jack Frost about
Don't scream or shout
He gets into your fingers and toes
Wherever he goes
The cool night air
Chills you to the bone
Shivering, we must go home
A drop of soup will warm us up
Steaming hot from the pot.

My Cat

'Tis, 'tis, what's that
You are indeed a fluffy cat
Up in the mornings
Without a warning
You are indeed Mr. Charming
You waggle, you bum
You lay on your tum
You are the one
You are the best
You are the one I love
More than the rest
So here it is, you're one of a kind
That I have in mind.

A Fresh Frosty Day

Jack Frost is about
Freezing my fingers and toes
He starts biting wherever I go
Ice all gleaming
Sparkling in the light
This is sure a delight
Pretty as a picture
Fresh as the dew
Cold outside and I feel blue
What a day it's been
Don't want to sound mean
It has been a day to remember
Forever and ever.

The Tale of a Christmas Tree

Christmas tree standing there
Long, tall as can be
Stars hanging one by one
Especially for me
Baubles pretty colors
Red, pink, white and gold
On the tree, tales to be told
Tinsel twisting round and round
Sparkling and glittering
Perched on the top
A big gold star
Not ready to drop.

Bath Time

Rub a dub-dub
You're in the tub
With a yellow duck
Sloshing around
All soapy and wet
To be dried off yet
Towel in hand
Mummy's best in the land
Drying me well
It sure is swell
Time for bed
A lot to be said.

Being There

The time has come to worship
To honor and pray
Time for us to lend a hand and help them
On their way
When all good things come to an end
We all need a jolly good friend
As time goes on, we count our blessings
For the sick and needy
We don't want to be greedy
As things plan out
We don't know whether to scream or shout.

A Jolly Christmas

A merry little Christmas
Church bells ringing
Yuletide a bringing
For the festive day
Hot mince pies
Sausage rolls a plenty
Bells on trees
Forgotten these
Drinks all around
Everyone's found
What fun it would be.

The Gathering

Creeping quietly as we can
On tiptoes, not to wake anyone up
Shhh! Must be quiet
Not to shout
We are having fun
Christmas has just begun
Hear footsteps moving about
Be alert, not in doubt
Decorations everywhere
All colors beware
Tinsel hanging about
What a picture
Get your cameras out
Noise all around
Talk about not making a sound
The toasting of glasses in the background I hear
Who's on the beer.

To Reflect

The day is over
Time has gone
A chance to remember
And to dwell on what's to come
Things change
And we arrange
Life goes on
And at this stage
Wonder how we carry on
To this day, there are no surprises
Wondering still whenever it arises
As we're all together and as one
We have each other
When others have none.

Waiting for Santa

Hoorah, hoorah
Christmas has come by far
Santa's on his way
Him and his sleigh
For this special day
With black boots and a beard
Something which is weird
All geared up and ready
Must keep the sleigh steady
Piled sky high
With toys galore
Delivering to people's door
A cold chill in the air
Snow dropping, so just beware
An echo far away
For the ending of the day.

Melting Ice

Snowflakes falling from the earth's core
Snowflakes melting forever more
A chilly feel from nature is real
Makes you think it's so unreal
Setting down all white and fluffy
Wet and absolute runny, very, very cold.

Snoozing

Snoring happily as can be
My little dog's the one for me
Laying there at peace
Wondering what's up at least
She Miss Charming, so she is
She has me in fits
Laying there for all to see
She's the happiest she can be
Loving and content
This is what's meant.

Having a Party

With prayers read
It's time for bed
Christmas day
Hip-hip, hooray
The festive season has just begun
We are all having fun
Celebrations to be had
We are all feeling glad
Children with Santa
Are having the time of their lives
This is to us a surprise
Each and everyone got a prize.

Flying Around the World

Up in the sky
I fly
Circling round
Up high
Spreading my wings as I go
Flapping them to and fro
The rushing of the wind
As I'm soaring by
All rustling my feathers
Till dark and nights nigh
And employees all around
Quiet as can be
Miles and miles
The world for you and me.

Loving You

Standing here alone I fear
You are always near
The very feel of your touch
Makes me realize how you're loved very much
A darling you are to me and the kids
All grown up now, I wonder how
Getting by all the time
Wonder how you were ever mine.

Adorable

Young and free
Beautiful as can be
Meek and mild
You're still a child
A warmth embraces you
Which amazes you
Can this be true
Or are you blue
So I will cheer you
And I will be near you.

A Joyous Day

Hark the herald the angels sing
Tonight's the night, let's begin
The bells are ringing out for Christmas day
So come on hurry, or it will be away
Far away the food is plenty
Come on now, it's all for the ready
Today's the day the Savior's born
So come on now, let's look to morn'.

Mum

Mother of mine
I love you so
You're the heart and soul of the show
You're there when needed most
You're always warm as toast
You're the rock that stands by me
Without thee, I am not free
In life we have a long way to go
You help me, I know that is so
It's now that you need me
And I will be there for thee.

What's Going On

Looking around, what do I see
A scruffy little world for which it's to be
The changes it's made are shocking, I know
It doesn't help with not having any dough
The rich and the poor
The meek and the mild
What comes down to it
It always concerns a child.

Clever Girl

Bright as a button
Likes her mutton
Hides her chops
Loves her pops
Christmas fun
Life has begun
Now for a feast
A meal at least
A queen of hearts
She loves her tarts
Always there when needed most
Can count on her
Don't need to boast
A lovable girl in my life
Better than my own wife.

A Noisy Night

Way up high
Floating by
Balloons a many
Cost more than a penny
Lots of colors
Wishes for them all
Let's have a ball
Fireworks by the number
Some want to have their slumber
Music loud
Everyone's proud
Playing through the night
A new year's delight.

Junior

Little one by far
You're my guiding star
Love you very much
You're heaven to touch
Amazed I am
To me, you're God's little plan
Your little fingers are busy
When you have us in a tizzy
Up all night
But that's alright
You have all your fun
When we're all glum
Children should be in bed
But enough said.

A New Dawn

Hark the herald
A new day has come
Ringing in the year
For which has not yet begun
2015 for us, we're here
Has come to bring us good cheer
Up and about the morning so early
Cats around and playing dirty
Little scamps they are
Wanted by far
They're the ones that are the best
Dog laying just like the rest.

The Trio

Standing to attention
One, two, and three
Pussycats marching for us to see
Two black and white
And one sandy
The cats that got the candy
All smug with a grin
Love the life on which they're in
Treated like kings and queens alike
I like to get out and go on my bike.

Relaxation

Snoozing happily in a chair
Wondering lightly, better beware
Up in the clouds I have gone
To infinity and beyond
A quiet moment it is indeed
One that I think I need
Gone are the stresses of the day
So relaxed in every way.

Us

Looking at you with a lovely smile
You and I have not been in touch for a while
Miles away from each other you and I
You in my thoughts as the days go by
Just like sisters, friends we're not
Mum and daughter is who we are
Been together through thick and thin
Life at the moment has just been grim
Struggling year by year
Now's the time we need some cheer
Remembering your father has brought you near
Life's not the same now, he's not here.

A New Day

With life so precious
Where will we be
The air that controls us
The wind blows free
Beauty all around us
Life's mapped out
Words cannot comprehend
What it's all about
Counting the days as season sets in
One, two, and three, now let spring begin.

My Baby

With a twinkle in her eye
She makes me cry
With love all over her face
Must take her at a slow pace
A smile so rare
Can't help but stare
With tight curly hair and blue eyes
She lays back and sighs
The day is gone
And for us now to carry on.

Time to Go

The flame of life
Flickers and dies
Then comes the time
We say our goodbyes
Called up from above
To the God that we love
Leaving our loved ones
And memories behind
Treasured and with
Thoughts that are kind
So as we slowly depart
We know within our hearts
Our journey is at an end
Goodbye to all our friends.

A Friend so True

With eyes of love
And a gift from God
I treasure this in my heart
A sign from you
I've been wondering what to do
My poems are new
So why am I blue
Missing you I think is true
God can help me in the things I'm to do
Guiding me on my way
I can only but try
Here's wishing that you were here
Keeping watch over me as time draws near.

Pests

Once you have it
That's what you got
You better scarper
Like it or not
Causing trouble that you do
Sometimes I wish that was not true
You're the cats that got the cream
Your little lives are nothing but a dream
Lovable so you are
You make me treasured by far
Spoilt to corruption
Didn't I mention
Without interruption
Your little direction
You're so sweet
I can tickle your feet
Loved to have you around
But I finally found
You can be too much for me.

Mates

Two little friends
Loving and giving
Frightened of what they're missing
Out to play one day
Their hearts not in it
What do you say
Been together a long time
Things going along fine.

My Lover

There was a man called Frances
Who always seemed to be in traces
He was clean-shaven, not rough
Very mild but not tough
He always whistled when going
Always there and worth knowing
When I'm wild
He treats me like a child
When I'm asleep, he takes a peep
He is always loving and giving
Works hard for his living
Nice to have around
And he's on the rebound.

Miserable Dog

With ears twitching
And looking very sad
My little dog is going mad
Not herself this morning
Came without a warning
Off her food you see
She will want to flee
Doesn't want to go
Has a mind of her own
Probably
Will have a moan.

Young at Heart

Looking at me
Staring away
You're the brightest youth of today
Appearing smart and looks to match
I think you're a very good catch
With brown wavy hair and eyes of blue
I sometimes think can this be true
A school boy you are
And young at heart
We will never be apart.

The Universe

Twinkle, twinkle
Little star
Up above the world so far
You're my brightest star of all
You twinkle day and night
And that's not all
Shining bright to my delight
For all to see until daylight
The stars out one by one
Twinkling till nighttime's done.

Lou Lou

Little cat
Graceful and pure
You're my one and only cure
You trot around with dainty feet
You're always there and looking neat
With little black paws
Mixed with white
You're the beautifulest cat of the night.

Sleep Walking

Up in the morning, asleep and alone
Wandering, not having a place to go
Silent as the night had been
Maybe this had been a dream
Quiet through the night
Tiptoeing with delight
Creepy and scary
Shivering to the core
As we go through the door.

Happy Dog

I look around and
What do I see
The dog wagging her
Tail and looking at me
Ears pricked back
Trying to hear
She's the monkey of the year
Rushing to the door
Tail dragging on the floor
Takes a look as to say:
'Come on, let's have some more
Walks on hand the best in the land.'

Relaxation

Drifting away
With not a word to say
Not a care in the world
Dreaming as it all comes together
It all has a meaning
Relax while you're sleeping
Dreaming away to your heart's content
This is what is sorely meant
Good for you in every way
This I can surely say.

Us

Drawn together
Now and forever
A family we are
Touched by a star
That's who you are
Wished by far
Missed so much
We all keep in touch
We come together in celebration
The very thought of you
Which makes us blue.

Kids

We laugh with glee
Us together makes three
Must keep in touch
Love them all so much
Have lives of their own
So I won't moan
Days are long
Must keep strong
Every time quiet
Must go on a diet
As life keeps going
We must keep the flame burning
As we remember the
Days that are gone
Life does go on
And we must carry on.

Playing a Match

Playing ball to and throw
This is how we catch our ball and go
Doing it week by week
We arrange it to meet
The fields are big
The lights are bright
Given the chance, we'll
Play it at night
Having been going for some years
We all went out to get some beers.

The Resurrection

Hark the herald
The bells are ringing
For the joyous day
To celebrate the birth
Of our Lord Jesus
Who was born today
The coming of the Lord
At this special time
As he is the first in line and the last
And remembered for all this.

My Hubby

With the love in your eyes
As we said goodbye
The tears that flowed
I wondered why
Missed so much
It tears me apart
Counting the days as we part
Remembering you softly within my heart
You're the dear, how did we start
Time goes on thinking of you well
Kids are fine and doing swell.

My Darling

With your loving smile
I'll be up in a while
Love you so much
Will keep in touch
Thoughts of you all the time
We're all fine
Time goes on
When you are gone
When you are near
Life is one big cheer
Happy to have you around
I treasure you and found
I cannot live without you.

Thinking On

Time's a ticking
Hearts are breaking
Life vanishing as we go on
Must keep going and be strong
Sitting here thinking and constantly wishing
It won't do us any good from now on
The years fly by
I won't tell a lie
Thoughts are with me every day
I get down on my knees and pray
Hoping that life will change in a way.

Being Dazzled

I look around me
And what do I see
Lights all about me
Bright as can be
Sparkling and twinkling
A shining sight
I am looking at it
With sheer delight
To me it's heaven
A feeling so right
Relaxed and serene
I feel thoroughly clean
A motion I feel
Is somehow real
Quiet and at peace
Warm at least.

Ringo

Lying there with not a care
Snoozing happily, must beware
The cat of my dreams
All handsome and gleams
Pure black and white
Sheer delight
A beautiful cat
Who sits on a mat
Purring to his heart's content
My old friend is who I meant.

A Mad Pooch

There was a poodle named Tiny
Who was very whiney
Kept everyone up at night
Gave the children a fright
Out in the morning
Without a warning
Everyone alert
Found him in the dirt
All scruffy and forlorn
Out in the early dawn.

One Night

Precious little baby, go to sleep
Mum's going to come and take a peep
Scrunched up curled up like a ball
Wonder if I get any sleep at all
Daddy's getting frantic
Prancing up and down
Mummy's sitting in a chair, making a frown
Up all night
Crying with all your might
Sleepless nights
Day until night
Tired are we
Must have tea.

Little Monkey

Little boy, you are my joy
With blond hair and big blue eyes
You've always got your finger in the pies
Into mischief so you are
Have to be watched or you'll go too far
Mummy loves you
You cheer her up
When she is blue
She would miss you so much
She wouldn't know what to do.

The Dead of Night

Stars so bright
Stars that twinkle through the night
Shining, glistening
In the moonlight
The moon stands out to my delight
A hoot of an owl in the distance
Perched on a tree hidden
From you and me
The eerie dark makes
It hard for us to see
Wind rustling through the trees
Making a lot of noise so it seems.

A Meeting

Standing there all
Scrummy and runny
Delicious chocolatey
And very funny
Decorated with Smarties and buttons
Wrapped in frills and flowers
Especially for baby showers
Loved by all
Let's have a ball
Tasty to eat
Where are we going to meet.

My Puss

My little tufty
Always very scruffy
A very, very fluffy, hairy little cat
Blind in one eye
A cross little guy
Cutest puss I ever had
With ears alert
Tends to flirt
With every lady and gent
Purrs a lot when content
Knows what fuss is meant.

Tammy

Little brown eyes
Looking up at me
With warm, rusty-brown fur
Lovely as can be
With love all over her face
Adorable to the day
She I will have around
Till the day I die
Greets you day and night
With absolute sheer delights
The greatest pooch in the world to me
My one and only.

My Son in Law

I know a man called Garth
Who is very daft
Has Mum in law up all night
Hoping things will go alright
Feels naff in the morning
After what went on without warning
Doesn't know what to do
She is feeling blue
Having met you
Things cannot be true
Haven't been here long
I of course can be in the wrong
Will things ever get sorted out
I would like to boot him about
Putting up with things has been tough
I of course feel rough.

A New Baby

Congratulations to you
This endearment is true
A lot of love goes with it
And kisses galore
Which I hope you will adore
All the loving and giving
Shows that I am willing from now and now on
The making of life is so precious
A wondrous little person to all
Warm, soft and cuddly
So keep calm and let life go on.

A Gliding Plane

The tree is tall
And that's not all
The birds sing
Flapping their wings
The kids about
Mummies want to shout
The dogs bark
In the park
The swans glide
Want to hide
A plane above
Flies down from the sky which is high.

A Party

Happy birthday to me
As I answer with glee
I look all around
And what do I see
Balloons above
And balloons below
On the tables and all over the show
Today I am so many years old
Something that you won't be told
Now I am free
It is time for tea
Now I wonder if you
Will come out with me.

My Man Ray

Inspired by Ray
My dish of the day
One of a few
His friends too
With hair of brown
Eyes of blue
He was a catch
A definite match
With a bristly beard
And a deep voice
He was a good choice
One thing I can say
He was great in his way.

A Jolly Poem

Run farmer, run farmer
Run, run, run
Do your best with your gun, gun, gun
Quick, run, what a rotten draw
You'll be better with the arm of the law
Come farmer, come farmer
You'll be late
You haven't ever shut the gate
All the animals are waiting in the yard
You have been kept off your guard.
Written with the song 'Run Rabbit Run' in mind.

An Eternal Love

You are my love for evermore
You will be the one I adore
Through thick or thin
You can be sure
We will just begin
You're the one
You're the baby
You're always there to drive me crazy
With the love in your heart
Mine put together
We will stay bonded
Forever and ever
You are my sunshine
You are my love
You are from heaven and the skies above
You are the heart of me
A part you will always own
You and I will never be alone.

A Cheerful Poem

Daisy
Darling Daisy
You bring happy days to skies of grey
I know, dear, that I don't doubt you
Don't take my true love away
The time has come, dear
You know what I mean, dear
Your beauty surrounds you every day
To me the love we show
Will go on forever
In the brightest, beautifulest way.
Written with the song 'You Are My Sunshine'
in mind.

A Trickster

Hear me, you old mucker
What a didler you are
You fiddle everybody from afar
You're up to your old tricks
And giving us some stick
Your absolute timing makes me sick
You drive me around the bend so much
I don't know whether I'm coming or going
But apart from that
You silly old bat
I love you.

The Visitor

You're heaven-sent
My child you're meant
So tiny, so small
You're wondrous at all
As you sleep
May we take a peep
For generations to come
My grandson, you're the one
Lying there, you look so sweet
I can't wait for you and I to meet
With all the blessing of an angel
Sleep, little one, sleep.

A Crying Baby

Sitting here with not a thought in my head
Wondering what I'm going to do instead
Another day
In a special way
Father would have been proud
Baby is wrapped and is loud
A new day to unwind
Here's hoping everyone is kind.

A Silent Night

Softly and silently, the crying stops
Ears alert in case he sobs
All is quiet
No soul awake in the house
Not even a mouse
No creaking of floorboards or squeaking of
  doors
Or goal's going about trying to shout
Just us tiptoeing to bed
Until morning instead.

Another Day

Nappies galore
Daddy upstairs
Having a snore
Mummy in the kitchen
Rattling the pans
The kids all disappearing, going to Nan's
The clock ticking by up on the wall
The birds outside giving a call
Sun's all out
Blue sky above
We're on a walk, which we just love.

A Busy Day

Pitter-patter of dainty feet
Tots on the landing
Wondering when we will meet
Crying, grizzling, having a paddy
Coming home soon will be Daddy
Tea's on the table
Coming around is Aunty Mabel
Chitchatting all day
Getting on with things in her way.

Family Prayer

Bless this house
My father to be
Living under the roof
Is what you will see
Working hard for my living
Providing for and always giving
Always around when needed most
Pardon me if I am not a host
I work so hard until I drop
Wearing myself out as I can't stop
My wife and children I love so much
Even now I have to touch
I can't believe that I have been blessed
The family, a unit and the rest
Altogether as one
Years from now we'll
Realize what we've done.

My Boy

My life, my joy
Lying there precious
An angel you are
You've been brought here from afar
God's gift
With which we are blessed
You're our little man
And you the best
Our two little boys are
The pick of the bunch
Darlings they are, we love them very much
All in all, when the day is done
Life goes on and we carry on.

A Beautiful Day

Birds singing in the trees
Squirrels darting in the leaves
A lovely day has begun
As we bring on the sun
The mid-morning dew
Fresh and crisp it is too
Lying here wondering what to do
I sure feel blue
The past few days have gone
We're wondering how to go on
Times have changed
Something must be arranged.

You Will Always Be My Rock

Loving you is easy
It happens every day
The love you bring surrounds me
In every sort of way
Always together
Joined forever
You're in my heart
You're in my soul
From now on, I have a goal
Although we will never part
You have given me a
Very good start
The love I cherish
The good times and the bad
Sometimes all this makes me rather sad.

Little Angels

Joshie and Tommy
Were two little boys
Not very big but loved their toys
Played in the garden, as good as gold
Joshie got a bit noisy
And had to be told
The two brothers were very good friends
Used to squabble until one gave in
Mum and Dad were
Proud as punch
Friends would come around
And have some lunch.

Having Fun

Everything goes out on a winter's night
The stars come out, which is sheer delight
The dark crisp cold of a morning
Chilly without a warning
Getting up early
A brisk walk first thing
A few steps later and
I start to sing
All cheered up and nowhere to go
Meeting the girls
Who are dressed just so
Now we're all ready
Let the music begin
Off to the nightclub
Where we will join in.

Looking On

Life has passed me by
I just want to cry
Thoughts of yesterday in my mind
Friends around me, which is kind
A lot has gone on through the years
Children have grown up
We have no fears
Looking around, what do I see
A lot of memories of you and me
As we close the door
Things change, don't seem to matter anymore.

Sizzling with Delight

Yummy, yummy it's all scrummy
Rolling around the pan
Sizzling to fill up my man
Sausages fried up one by one
Which one shall we pick
They're all tough and thick
Juicy and nice
I won't think twice
We're all at the table
I'll get the radio and cable
Turn on and play
We'll eat without delay.

Leaving a Parcel

Pong-pong, sniff-sniff
Let's all go and have a whiff
The smell is high
I want to sigh
Too much for me
I have to flee
A cat sneaks out
From where he's been about
With a look of surprise, we're all wise
Now we got the culprit
And the devil is caught.

Buddies

Tuffy and Ringoli
Are two little cats
Dozing in a dog bed
Being lazy instead
With nothing to dream about
One was the king of the cats
Who lorded over them
There were scrapes
Always having naps
Hungry for food
Whenever they were in a mood
Some characters were they
Moving in the hay
Little buggers they say.

Butterflies

My time is over
I learn to fly
Flapping my wings
As a butterfly
In the night air
I flap about with flair
Joining another in an act of despair
Twisting and turning
We move around
High up in the sky
I sourly found
Looking at things to settle on
Leaves of green
With all wet on
Juicy and nice
I don't think twice.

The Final Days

A dog is forlorn
Looks at me until dawn
With sad, droopy eyes
And longing of goodbyes
Up and about
Not knowing what to do
It sure is hell and making me blue
Waiting for a knock
A person waiting will be a shock
Laying all cold, I cover her up
And then I'm told
Her final days are numbered
Best to let her go
The vet has finally told me
So now I know.

Darling Daughter

Smoochy-poochy
Pudding and pie
You're the girl for me
That's no lie
Snuggling up all warm and cozy
You're my little one and
I will call you Rosie
As you go to sleep
I have a good weep
To think you are mine
Loving you is just fine
As you grow up
I will get you a pup
For your very own
As you have always known.

Artful Dodger

Tinker, tinker
You little stinker
You're smelly as can be
I want to flee
You bring on a tear
So I don't want to be near
I feel so sad
You make me mad
A loving little dog
A great little friend
Even though you drive me around the bend
A biscuit-eater you are
Full of greed, that's for sure
Yours eyes pop out
Where they're about
Sneaky as can be
It's gone before I can see.

Being Together

Love's so precious
A wondrous thing
All warm and beautiful and tingling
So very special
Makes your heart sing
With all the joys it brings
As two people come together
Their worlds simply fall apart
Two hearts are joined
They're on to a new start.

One So Precious

You're a little pickle
I'll give you a tickle
You lay there for all to see
Your face is so full of glee
A little darling to thee
You are one of a three
Your smile is so precious
I could eat you
You look so delicious
You're beautiful as can be
The loveliest kid you are
And thank God you have come to thee.

My Lovable Yorkie

For you, dear dog
You're heaven-sent
Always there whenever you're meant
You come to me with a look of sadness
This makes me feel a lot of gladness
You're so warm with your dear little eyes
So many times you don't like goodbyes
A rock to me you have been for so long
You deserve a great big gong
My beautiful girl you will always be
The cutest little one
You ever did see.

A Quiet Moment

Sitting there
Having a big stare
The smile on your face
Thinking of time going at a pace
The noise of a ticking clock on the wall
Pictures hanging in the hall
Ladies chitchatting in dining room
Music playing, going off with a boom
The humdrum day of a busy house
Nothing scary, not even a mouse
A lot of helpers rushing around
Nothing to show for it, not even a pound.

Christmas Day

A plumped-up turkey
Laid on a plate
All oozing with grease
What a messy state
Table laid food a plenty
All lined up and dainty
Cake on table
Tall as can be
Three times up
As you can see
Everyone having fun
The festive time has begun
The hall is full
A cracker, one for all.

Little Tubby Chops

Grumble, grumble
Little girl
You're the one who hides
Behind her tail
Your ears prick up
Hoping with any luck
Anything from a tin to a pig's ear
To give glad tidings for the year
All snuggled up
Ready to pop
A right fat belly
So give us some welly
You're the girl with all the charm
Come on now, you mean no harm
Our darling of the day
Sweetness in every way.

My Precious, Precious Baby

A lovable mutt
You like to lick your butt
Brown and white in color
You're the one we always favor
The runt of the litter
I've yet to twitter
You're my baby
A fine little lady
You're so sweet
I can't wait till we meet
A walk in the morning
The sun shining
A new day has begun
Let's have some fun.

A Sweet Little Lady

The smiley look upon your face
To me, dear dog, you look ace
You sit there and grin
You smile within
The best little Yorkie ever seen
We never know where you have been
Up to tricks I've no doubt
You always keep away when I shout
The cutest lassie I ever knew
You're always around even if I'm blue.

The Colors of a Rainbow

Fields are green
Sky is blue
Here I am
Loving you
The clouds are white
Yet to be seen
Sometimes later
Maybe in a dream
Miles away is a rainbow
Lots of colors
Starting with blue
Always very true
Because I am with you.

A Scrap

Counting colors one to ten
All lined up now and then
Bright ones, dull ones, just to name
Now we can start this fire game
Every morning when we wake up
My brother and I have a shake-up
We wrestle each other
And get into bother
Our mum comes in and starts off another
An argument breaks out, we have a shout
Dad comes in and wonders what it's about.

Hunted

Foxes, foxes on the run
Farmer following behind with his gun
Through the woodland they sure go
Not exactly going slow
Dogs follow farmer
His gun out, ready to strike
Makes the foxes do a hike
Into the river they fled
Maybe will catch a pike instead.

The Fattest Pig in Town

Little piggy porker
Was a great big stalker
With big goggly eyes
And with a disguise
All covered in dirt
Has everyone out on alert
Always going miles
Getting himself lost
No matter what the cost
This pig was special
Once a year entered in a show
Top pig on the go
Everyone liked to know
Was the talk of the town
And nobody thought of putting him down.

In Festive Spirit

Mince pies galore
Enough for one and all
Not a bore
Would like some more
The party begins
Everyone sings
Joyous to all
We shall have a ball
Christmas is here
We bring good cheer
Celebrations go on
Time to be strong
We all reunite
Which is polite
Thoughts of others
Including our mothers
The Lord has spoken.

Little Miss Artful

Foxy, foxy
All furry and nice
You don't have to look twice
You sure is good looking
You like my cooking
Especially off our plate
Even when it's late
You sit there goggle-eyed
Hoping someone will take pity on you
The sweetest little dog are you
Always there when we are blue.

Queen of Cats

Oh hungry eyed I am
Quite honestly, I don't give a damn
Every morning I'm about
Nagging my owner, except I can't shout
I can't lie like other cats in a chair
I'm always up, so they had better beware
I meddle with the TV
I jump up on all the cupboards
But most of all
I'm simply gorgeous
Purring is not my middle name
It's just that I'm always on the game.

Getting Ready

Daisy, Daisy
I'm always lazy
Things left when needed
Put away not far
I am certainly not a star
My dusting days are over
I'd rather be in clover
Every excuse that I can make
I would get out of it for pity's sake
Tidying up is second on the list
This is taking the Mick
Can't say I like laying in the sack
But I like a jolly good pack.

Up to Trouble

You are a minx
You have been a jinx
A swirl kind of girl
Who is in a whirl
You party all day long
You don't know where you belong
You're dizzy
Absolutely in a tizzy
You're totally drunk
You're looking for somewhere to bunk
What a mess you are
Trouble always follows
You, that's for sure
When it comes down to, it you're a bore
But you're always back for more.

My Ginger Tom

My old cat
Is a fuss pot
Worries you whether you
Want him or not
Always there on hand
Thinks he is in command
Keeps you on your toes
In your way wherever he goes
A lovely cat he is
Misses you to bits
Drives you up the wall
Especially when you got a call
Where will you be without him
Miss him, his name is Tim.

A Doggie Crowned

A smile on your chops
You're great, you're tops
Miss doggy of the year
Now that Christmas is here
We will bring out the beer
To give good cheer
On this day in every way
Talked about every day
Chitchatting so they say.

King of the Cats

You shake from side to side
Getting ready to turn and hide
A gentle purr comes from your lips
As when I am with you
My heart does flips
The coolest cat I do love
The gentle giant from above
You gather together with pride
Looking at the shed inside
Purring away
Ready for a sleep for the day.

A Day to Remember

Rise and shine
We're all be fine
The day is new
And simply are few
Blue skies we hope
This we can cope
A silence is peaceful
Forever restful
What's around the corner
We shudder to think
If we're careful, we'll
Be in the pink.

Thoughts of Today

You sit and stare
As if you don't care
The look in your eyes
Makes you truly wise
A big man you are
Guiding like a star
When you were around
You were a warm kind of guy I found
Missing you so
Can't help it, I know
No one to blame
It would just happen the same
Life is so unfair
Taking risks, you better beware
Forgetting all the tears
Time will get better over the years.

Swimming Gracefully

There was a fishy-lishy
That lived in a dishy
Swimming happily around
Up and down on the rebound
Night after night, he swam
In the cool always on
Show for one and all
This little fishy had one thing on his mind
If anyone was kind
A mate would be fine.

The Joining Together

Today's the day
We celebrate in our way
The church bell rings
The choir sings
The voices are heard
As we have the last word
We all come together
In a congregation-whatever
To welcome the birth of the Lord
The people unite
For all their might
Rejoicing throughout the world.

Homeward Bound

It is twilight
Everything is bright
We all snuggle together
With all our might
Silence for all
Just the sound of crackling under foot
We are not very tall
As we stand back against the wall
It's all creepy
We mustn't do a weepy
As we struggle to get home
We have no phone
Everyone's asleep
Must have been counting sheep.

Going to a Party

You wiggle and wiggle
My little pickle
Snuffly you go
You like to bow
You look sweet
And you dress so neat
With blonde pigtails
And a frilly little dress
Sometimes I think you look a mess
You stand there all innocent
You don't know what is meant
You wish you went
Everyone had gone
Even the dog had gone along.

Jumping Out

Sneaky-peaky
You're all creepy
Up all night
You give me a fright
You creep around
Making no sound
Is this a wind-up
Can't you make your mind up
I shiver from top to toe
As you're always causing me woe
And you're always treading on my toe
Last but not least, you're the beast.

The Unwrapping of Presents

Christmas is all over
And we're all in clover
Presents had by all
Kids driving you up the wall
Crowds and crowds of children about
Lots of screaming and shouting
Mums and dads don't know which way to go
They are always slow
Chatting to each other to pass the day
A cheer or two as we go on our way.

A Windy Day

With wind blowing through the locks
Worse than it looks
Must get out the books
A good reader I am
I'll get my sandwich out with ham
A drink to follow
On my way tomorrow
Hoping for a good day
Something special may be coming my way
Another day begins
So hopefully, everybody wins
The raffles shared out
I'm an early riser and about.

Going on Her Travels

Sleepy Sue
Doesn't know what to do
Up all morning
To music without warning
A smile on everybody's faces
Cheers her up
So she get her cases
A big day ahead
So mustn't forget the time instead
Offered a tea early on
Now she must be gone
She is now ready, although unsteady
As everybody says goodbye
She gets out her hanky and has a cry.

Down in the Dumps

With rain in the air
I'm full of despair
The days are long
Have to carry on
Maybe listen to a song
Everything quiet
Not even a mouse
Must go on a diet
Otherwise I'll be the size of a house
Every day comes and goes
Keeps me on my toes
Always busy
Don't want to get dizzy.

Another Year to Remember

A new year has begun
The millennium for everyone
A milestone once a year
Along with it to bring us cheer
Celebrations all around
Fireworks get to be found
The ringing of the year
With our loved ones so dear.

Tam the Greatest

You're the mouse
As big as a house
We call you Titmouse
Always snorting
Always licking
Sniffing where you like
Up to tricks
Picking up sticks
You always find
And we don't mind
But we love you with all our heart
For it's now we can never part
There's one thing for sure
It's you we adore
The biggest hound we
Applaud for more.

My Other Half

Dear heart
The love of my life
Don't forget I'll always be your wife
For richer and poorer
In sickness and in health
You and I have never had wealth
Have followed you through the years
Counting the fags and the beers
But most of all, we got on so well
The troubles that followed
Sort out I did
When it comes down to it
You are a kid
But deep down, I loved you so
Every time I was near you
You made me glow.

Start of a New Year

Shake the drawers clean
Making the window gleam
Thinking about the future
A new year has come
A clean sweep to be done
An explosion of twelve
Fireworks to celebrate
What a change the year would make
So for heaven's sake
Let the party begin
And then we will win.

Said in a Heated Moment

You're a git
What a twit
Even though you're a nit
Thought of it a special way
Twisted my words to what they say
The laughter we had just
Doesn't go away
We are so close
It's hard to imagine
What a guy you are
You're my treasure, that's for sure.

A Daft Fellow

Here you are, prick
What a dick
You wobble your bum as
If you don't care
Whenever I'm around you
You don't dare
For you have dust in your hair
Flicked over in such a way
All punky and gay
The perfect bloke in town
The one with a bent half a crown.

My Mother-in-Law

You're a dragon I even did encounter
You're the mother-in-law
I ever wonder
But deep in my heart, you're a saint
To this day I can't wait
As I walk in a chill
Meet the air
I needn't worry as I
Know I have to beware
You're the woman who cares
To this day it's okay
We come to see you
Without delay.

So He Lives to See Another Day

Little mousey
In a housey
Scurrying away
Disappearing for another day
His head's popped out
A cheese he smells
Out comes the cat
Claws out to pounce
Everything comes down
Every ounce
The cat looks around in despair
Where is the mouse, he had better beware
He slumps off to a corner for a snooze
Imagining everything, even the mouse on the booze
Disappointed so that day
Hopefully, tomorrow will go his way.

Trusting God

It's a beautiful day
I hold my hands up and pray
Thank God every morning
Bow down to him without warning
He is waiting I say
Follow him every way
The seasons come and go
The years fly by as you know
As life goes on
And our dreams become real
Time will tell, as we had a good deal.

At War

Soldier, soldier, marching along
Gun in hand, singing a song
A troubled war breaking out
Running around, everybody shout'
Tanks moving on, creaking as they go
All stiff and old
Men shaking as if cold
Living on nerves do they
Can't wait till the end of the day
Men are either alive or dead
Wish they were with their wives instead.

Prince of All Pussy Cats

Pussy and pussycat
Meow, meow, meow
Laying down in the grass
Calmly bold as brass
Wondering and dreaming of fish
In a huge round dish
All smooth and white
Sheer, pure delight
Soft to the touch
Love him very much
Smothers me in affection
Every time I mention
He's the beautifulest
Puss in the world
So clever I'm told.

End of the Road

On a slipping road to hell and back
There's no longer a turning on to track
The final journey
A one last goodbye
Time has gone
I want to cry
The years I have missed
Everything has a twist
Everywhere I look seems to be a mist
All I remember is being let down and ignored
No wonder I was always bored
So if there is a God up there
I wonder if he will even care.

Reckless

Out for mischief, into trouble
You go after those who are gullible
You're the nuisance of this world
We have to make a stand and be bold
The innocent suffer
Which is wrong
You drive reckless'
Leaving everyone legless
You're the menace who must be stopped
Must be caught by the arm of the law
Locked up and throw away the key.

Chances

Taking chances every day
Sometimes work out in some small way
As we work ourselves in time
Every dream comes in line
A dream comes true in our mind
Made up of everything I find
It turns out unreal
But we like to think it happened still
In our lives, we have to make our luck
If it happens, we make a buck
Things don't just fall into our laps
We have to earn them or have a relapse.

It Is So You

Sugar and spice
You're everything nice
Sweetness and light
You're a delight
Your lips are red
All plumped up instead
All tasty and sweet
Could do with something to eat
You are swell
Forget the smell
Lavender so blue
With a scent so true.

My Little Tufty

You look at me with a look so rare
Your eyes so bright, they cause a glare
You have a smirk all over your face
Next when I look, there isn't a trace
Deadly shocked I am to see
You're the one and only for me
Ginger-looking fluffy to boot
You're the one who does not care a hoot
The nicest puss of all
You'll soon be jumping over the wall.

One of the Best

You lay there hunched up on the seat
All snug and cozy, ready to meet
Ears pricked back and purring like mad
In you there is nothing bad
A heart like an angel
You're one of a kind
You always make a pass with me in mind
An adorable creature that you are
I will always like you the most
You lay on my legs and
Keep me warm as toast.

Two Great Friends

Tammy and Simba are two of a kind
Two little dogs with a big heart in mind
Been together for so long
Never did anything wrong
Trusting, loyal
Always in for a spoil
Simba, who has a black and white coat
With a ginger tinge
He was always the one to have a binge
Tammy, a Yorkie who is so porkie
Loves a fuss
And going on a bus
Great little friends they are
Love going about in a car.

Mr. Tittle Mouse

Crawling and turning around
The young mouse is playful I found
Fast he does run
Up to tricks, he has fun
On the go all the time
Can't keep up but that's all fine
Keeps away from mousetraps
All you find is mouse craps
Mouse likes the cheese
When he sees the, cat he just freezes.

A Blustery Day

Waves swishing against the wall
Some are high, some are tall
A cold wind hits the beach
Blowing around things it can't reach
Beach umbrellas flapping about
This bitter snap nips at your feet
Friends arranged, we don't meet
A blue sky brightens up
Lighting everything around
A total transformation I found
A fresh air hits you
Cold to the touch
A great day this morning
I love it very much.

A Charmer

Lying there, a babe in arms
You're the one with all the charms
All sweet and cute
You're a little beaut
All soft and cuddly
A little wriggler you are
A little pickle by far
When you cry
There is a big sigh
Mother's not far away
Milk is on its way.

A Doggy Tale

Lying there so sweet and calm
I want to keep you safe from harm
You're the sweetness in my life
You're the baby of my life
You keep me going forever more
You are the one I adore
Cute as can be
You're the one for me
I love having you around
You're groovy and you're sound
Together we belong
You're my doggy friend all along.

On a Date

You sit there proud as punch
I could almost take you to lunch
Sitting in a chair with an air of I don't care
Playing hard to get
Something I didn't expect yet
The lads all standing, watching
The ladies all ready and waiting
With a shrug and a hard up look
I disappear to read a book.

Remembering the Times

Remember when our lives began
You and I were the same back then
Frightened of our own shadows
Going for walks down grass meadows
Life was good
When you were in the mood
Worked till you drop
Now you're a gran pop
Your smoking days are over
No drinking you do
You're a hell of a lot healthier
Although not wealthier
You're the string attached to my bow
I love you so.

Keeping up the Beat

Policeman Plod
You're a very nice sod
Up early in the morning
On the beat without warning
Plodding everywhere
Catching criminals if you dare
Whistling away
Happy to the day
You're the taskmaster behind the force
Wondering when to take the course.

Wishing You Were Here

Without you
I feel blue
You just haven't a clue
Day and night
I'm up till light
You I know was my delight
As time flies, I ask why
Sitting down, I long to cry
As the sun comes out
And the clouds drift by
A bright light catches my eye
A warmth overwhelms me
I know that I am free
But in my heart
You're my soulmate to thee.

Out and About

We jog merrily on our way
With not a word to say
Headphones dangling in our ears
Thinking about those beers
Puff-puff as we go
Jogging until we say so
With bottle in hand
The best in the land
Water trickling down
A big thirst I found
On my face a frown
While listening to the sound
Making way for home as I am alone.

Great Nan

You're a granny
You're always listening to tranny
As deaf as can be
You're a great host to me
What a goer
You couldn't go any slower
Having reached a ripe old age
You like to read every page
Every morning
Without warning
A newspaper
You sleep all day
Worn out I say.

Two Brothers

Joshua and Tommy
Are two of a kind
They're my grandsons and both under nine
Lovely boys so they are
They're so charming, they are a star
Tommy cries so much
He's one of a bunch
Joshua's the one wanting his lunch
All in all, they get on well
My two grandsons are simply swell.

Shower Time

A scruffy little urchin, that you are
A rub and powder will suit you I'm sure
You line up ready to go
You don't want to be slow
You all march in, ready to begin
Shower gushing
Everybody rushing
Some whistle to their heart's content
Some bend down with their legs bent
Soap passes from one to another
Towels are ready to smother
Bath time is at an end
I think this can become a trend.

Time to Wind Down

I am knackered
So very cream-crackered
Tired and worn out as can be
Done too much
Must have some lunch
Have a brunch
Then I'll be free
To have some tea
Rest as much as I can
Must fill up a pan
Boiling away
Eggs ready I say
A dippy egg for the day
Everything going my way.

Playing Football

Running around on a pitch
Puffing about with a stitch
Little men run
Red and blue
And having fun
The ball passes from one to another
Half of me here and the rest to my mother
Standing by the goal
This is better than being on the dole
A ball goes by my legs
Making me do the splits
And jumping out of my wits.

A Crazy Night

Drinking with mates
Going on dates
Turning up late
Can't always wait
Girls waiting for a night out
All they do is fool about
On the razzle they are
Drink in hand
Guzzling as they command
The ladies always in demand
Shout and they carry on
This is the night from now on.

A Letter to a Valentine

You are my Valentine
You are my joy
You are my one kind of boy
When we begin
You are my sin
All tall and dark
You don't even leave a mark
Sunshine and roses
All I need is posies
On this one special day
All I need is you I say
The stranger of my dreams
Thinking about you, I come
Out of my seams
But all in all, the love
We feel today
Will carry on this way.

Dedication in Verse

My beloved sweetie
Forever we meet
Up and yonder
The miles we wander
You're the darling of my life
I thank God you are my wife
To me, you are the best
And you always make the test
Dear one
Now that life has begun
And we have had our fun
You are my soulmate and my joy
You stayed by me and gave me a boy
To me, my darling, you mean the world.

My Darling Yorkie

Pretty, pretty as can be
You're the little girl for me
Looking huffy and in a mood
You have gone for a snooze
With ears pricked back
You fancy a snack
Looking down in under attack
You deserve a whack
Pulling at my sock
So they come off
Up to tricks
You love your treats
You're the dog who nicks the sweets
When it comes down to it, you're the best
You are better than the rest.

Losing My Temper

To me I mumble
Forever I grumble
Cross as can be
Got my gander up you see
Wound up alright
To their sheer delight
Ready to blow
They will surely know
As my cross patch ends
All I want to be is friends.

A Chocoholic

Chocolate is tasty
Chocolate is sweet
Chocolate is a delight to eat
All wrapped up, ready to go
Can't wait to dive in and not too slow
Savor the moment as it slowly melts
It was heaven-sent
I sure know how it felt
A lovely, smooth taste to enjoy
A wonderful thing to share with a boy.

A Proposal

You are my Valentine
You are my love
You take me to dine
We have some wine
You're a great mate of mine
Been together for so long
Wonder where we go from there
Everyone has a jolly good stare
On your knees you do go
Hands out, ready to make a show
With a ring in hand
The words follow as if in command
A wonderful night to my delight.

Mummy's Little Baby

My little girl
A sweetheart you are
You're the love of my life
And the best by far
Laying there all fluffy and curly
With a look in your eye
Wondering why I'm so early
Upset your routine, that's for sure
You're sniffing about and looking for more
Having had your meal
You look at me as if unreal
Now the morning's here
We can have some cheer.

Missing You

Tiny, tiny Titmouse
You're the one around the house
The sweetest dog of all
We can now have a ball
Misses so much since
I've been away
Can't wait to come
Home and have my say
All brown and fluffy
Can see you're all huffy
Missing me all the time
You would like to have a good whine
One thing I know
You're quite a girl.

My Big Brother

Joshua and Tommy
Having fun
Have a bond that'd just begun
Always together whenever it be
Get on fine just you see
Big brother Josh is a
Great one to know
He is always on the go
Up to tricks is he
He always wants to flee.

I So Happy

Tammy, a mouse you are
You toddle about like a little star
You're the best, it's true
You're the one for me when I'm blue
The sun comes out
And you're about
A wonderful dog I shout
You wag your tail in greeting
I can't wait for a meeting
You're a swell girl
Whom I could twirl.

My Darling

You are my honeybee
You smell divine
You're perfect all the time
I of course have to keep you in line
You're my darling I fear
You've always been a dear
Thought of so dearly
Got away with it so cheaply
But wonderful you are
You've been a star
Couldn't have done things without you
Sometimes I wonder if this could be true
For there are times when you make me blue
But I will always need you.

A Dog up to Mischief

There in the corner so dear
A mutt who always gives me cheer
The look on your face
Overwhelms me at a pace
With the look of fear
You have me near
A feeling of sadness
Knowing you're still with me
There is a gladness
So very much loved
Can't believe my luck
You're always in the muck
You're in the water like a duck.

Fondly Remembered

The wisest of the lot
You're my dad who's loved
And who I got
Thought of so dearly
Missed so much really
Miss the times you potter
About in the shed
Most of the time, you don't go to bed
Making so much noise, you do
Up the stairs
I hear you go to the loo
Everyone knows when you're about
You always seem to want to shout.

Grandfather

I dream of you
You dream of me
We belong together passionately
Smoochy and smooch-woo
There are a hundred things to do
All huddled up and so complete
We don't want to admit defeat
Many years, our feelings grown
Together we have had children of our own.

A Little Cherub

Little miss sunshine
The sweetest child in all the world
With blonde curly looks
And a smile so rare
You're so little I do declare
A loving little girl
Who walks with style
Gets up to tricks
Plays about with sticks
Naughty but nice
Never thinks twice
As cute as can be
What would life be like without thee.

Roli

A sweet puss you are
Eyes out on stalks
You're the one who talks
We sit and stare
We know you are there
The one to be proud of
You think you know it
We sure do show it
You push our button
And get what you want
The king of the house
Is what you are
You of course are our little star.